CLASSICAL REMIX FOR THE RECORDER

by DAMON CARTER

Song Selections Arranged by Damon Carter for DC Music Lab

Backing Tracks Produced and Arranged by Damon Carter for DC Music Lab

Cover Design by Jan Carlo Dela Cruz

Book Design and Graphics by Charylu Roberts (orubyproductions.com)

ISBN 978-1-7368832-0-4

How to Use This Book

First and foremost, I'd like to thank you for purchasing *Classical Remix for the Recorder*. The vision for this book began with me occasionally recording piano accompaniments for my recorder students to use for practice. These recordings soon evolved into full band tracks making students the featured performers backed up by professional musicians! Then I got the idea to create a song book with easy arrangements of Classical pieces, of course, with backing tracks.

Before exploring this adventure in recorder and Classical music, the student should have a metronome. The tempo of each piece is set to match the backing track tempos. If you don't own a metronome, free metronome apps are available for download on the iTunes App Store. I recommend Smart Metronome and Tuner. Scan the QR code with the camera app of a phone or tablet to access the app.

Be sure you are using a soprano recorder with Baroque fingering—not German. There are two indicators for a Baroque recorder:

1) A letter "B" engraved above the thumb hole.

2) The right-hand finger hole number 1 is small and the hole for finger 2 is large. *CRTR* can also be used with any treble clef concert pitch instrument.

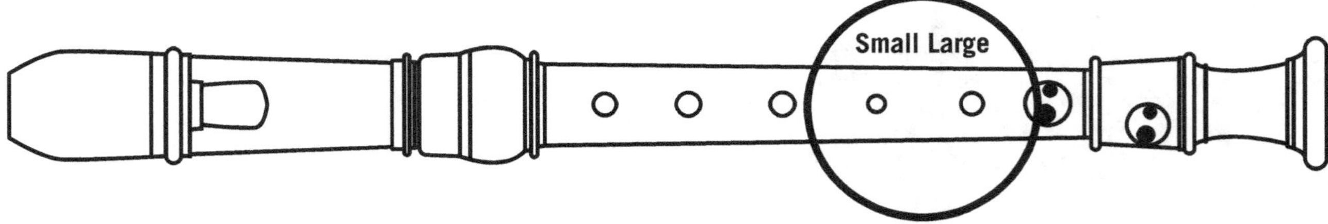

Classical Remix for the Recorder (CRTR) is not intended to be used as a detailed recorder method, though instruction is provided on how to practice each piece. *CRTR* works best when used as a performance repertoire book for recitals or concerts. Practice each piece in 4 measure increments until you can play them from beginning to end. Additionally, students are introduced to new notes, short bios of the composers, and fast facts about each piece. You can access the backing tracks by scanning the QR code with the camera app of a phone or tablet. Finally, you are free to randomly select any piece you want to learn. The pieces are arranged in order of easiest, "Moonlight Sonata," to most challenging, "Winter."

CLASSICAL REMIX FOR THE RECORDER

Contents

DC MUSIC LAB

MOONLIGHT SONATA

Ludwig Van Beethoven (1770–1827)

The original title of this piano sonata is "Quasi Una Fantasia Op. 27, No. 2."
The piece was later nicknamed "Moonlight Sonata" after Beethoven's death.
The first movement is described as a metaphor for moonlight because of its
haunting mood.

With Recorder, track 1
Recorder muted, track 2

Ludwig Van Beethoven
Arranged by D. Carter

Slow Gospel

Image • arcady31 © 123RF.com

Warm up

♩ = 46

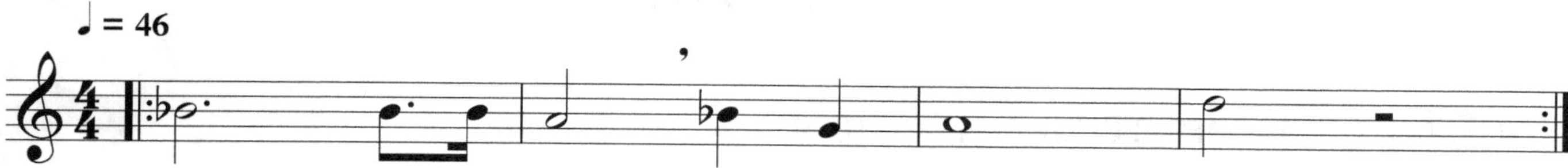

MOONLIGHT SONATA

First play each note in the fingering diagram several times to become familiar. Set metronome to 4/4 time. Practice warm up and piece at 46 tempo. Breathe in enough air to sustain the dotted half, and whole notes. Follow the breath marks (’) and blow even and relaxed air. All the Bs are played as B♭ in the warmup.

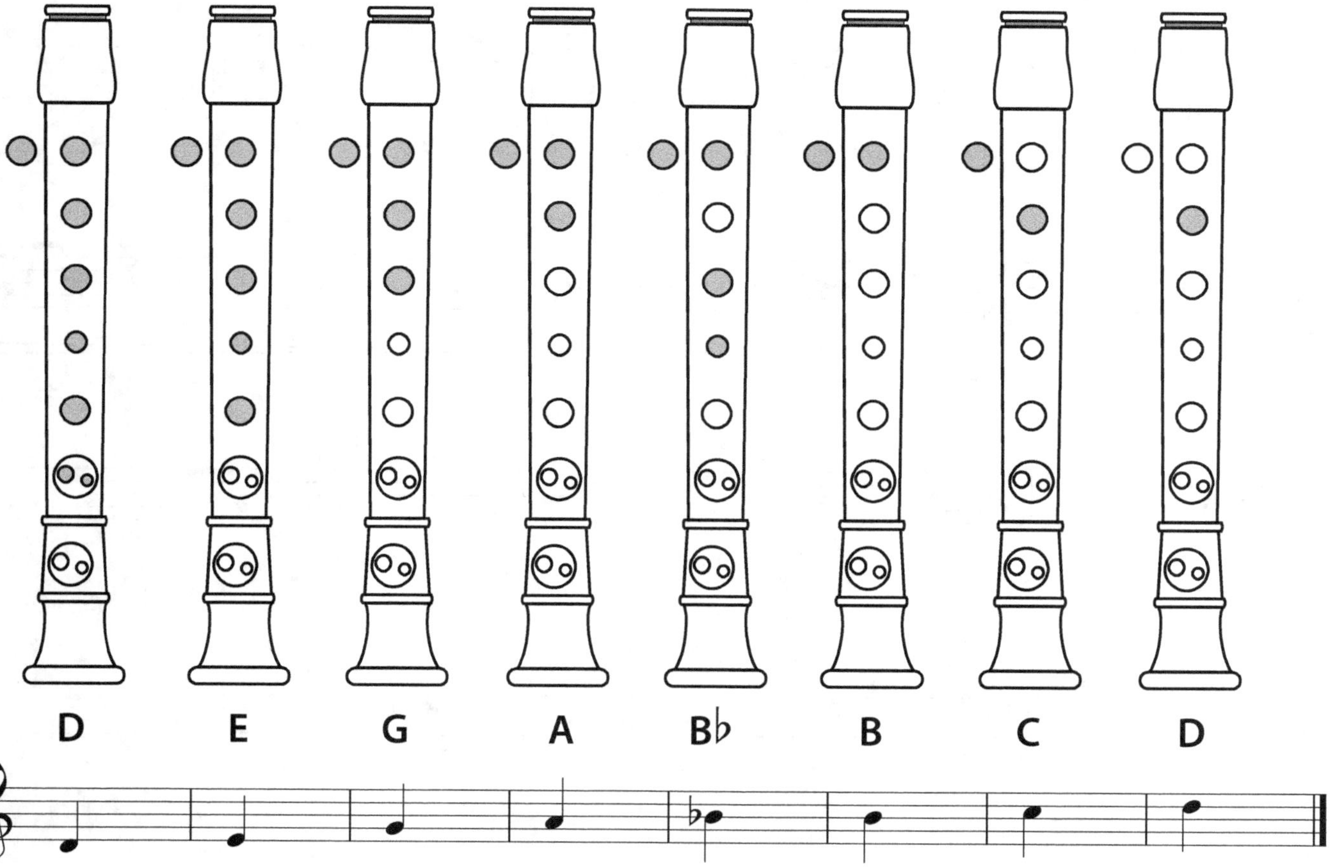

PRELUDE OP. 28, NO. 4

FRÉDÉRIC CHOPIN (1810–1849)

"Prelude Op. 28, No. 4" was one of 24 preludes composed by Chopin. He suffered from chronic illness which may explain why the piece channels emotions of sadness and despair to the listener. Chopin requested "Prelude Op. 28, No. 4" be played at his own funeral.

With Recorder, track 3
Recorder muted, track 4

Frédéric Chopin
Arranged by D. Carter

Jazz Ballad

♩ = 57

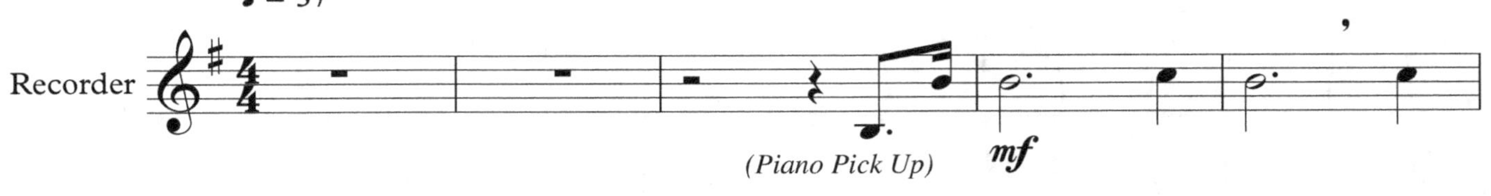

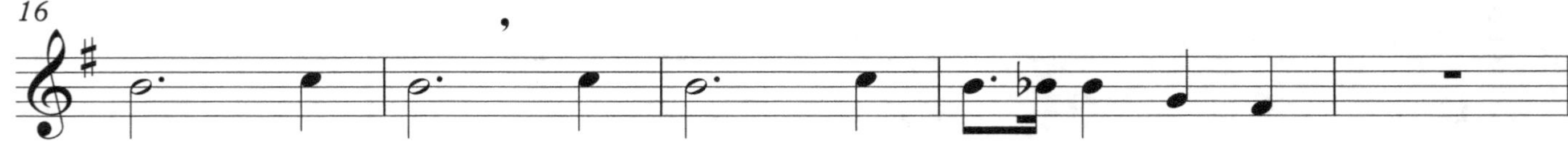

This Arrangement Copyright © 2021 DC Music Lab
International Rights Sercured   Made in U.S.A.   All Rights Reserved

Image • Georgy Borozdkin © 123RF.com

Warm up

PRELUDE OP. 28, NO. 4

First play each note in the fingering diagram several times to become familiar. Set metronome to 4/4 time. Practice warm up and piece at 57 tempo. Breathe in enough air to sustain the dotted half, and whole notes. Prelude is in the key of E minor. Every F is played as F sharp. Follow the breath marks (') and blow even and relaxed air.

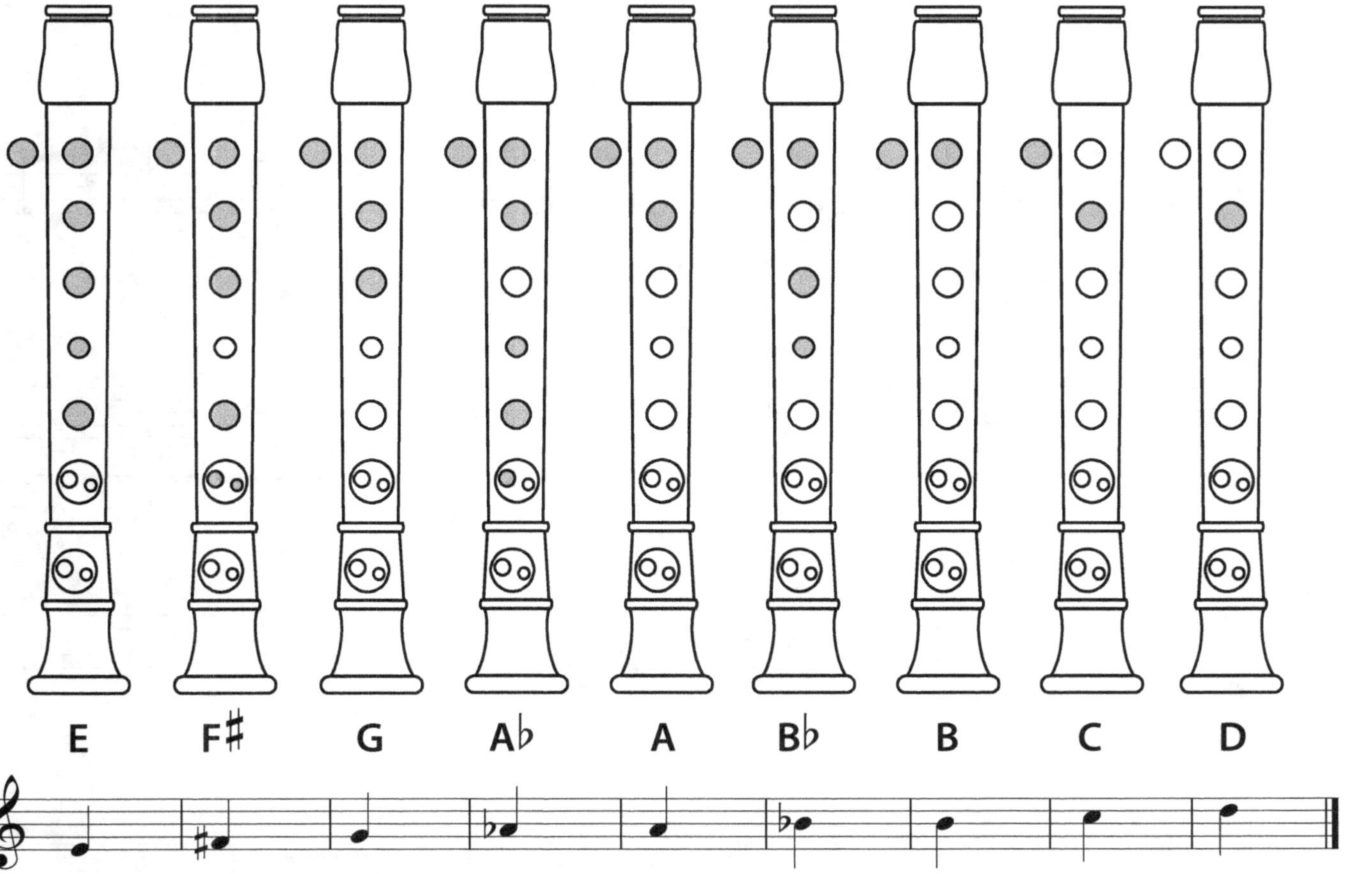

EINE KLEINE NACHTMUSIK

Wolfgang Amadeus Mozart (1756–1791)

Mozart composed "Eine Kleine Nachtmusik" in 1787. The opening melody is perhaps the most familiar theme of all time in Classical music.

With Recorder, track 5
Recorder muted, track 6

W. A. Mozart
Arranged by D. Carter

Image • Georgy Borozdkin © 123RF.com

EINE KLEINE NACHTMUSIK

First play each note in the fingering diagram several times to become familiar. Notice the many skips in the melody. Set metronome to 4/4 time. Practice warm up and piece at 50 tempo. Slowly work your way to 68 tempo. "Eine Kleine" is in the key of F major. Every B is played as B♭. Follow the breath marks (') and blow even and relaxed air.

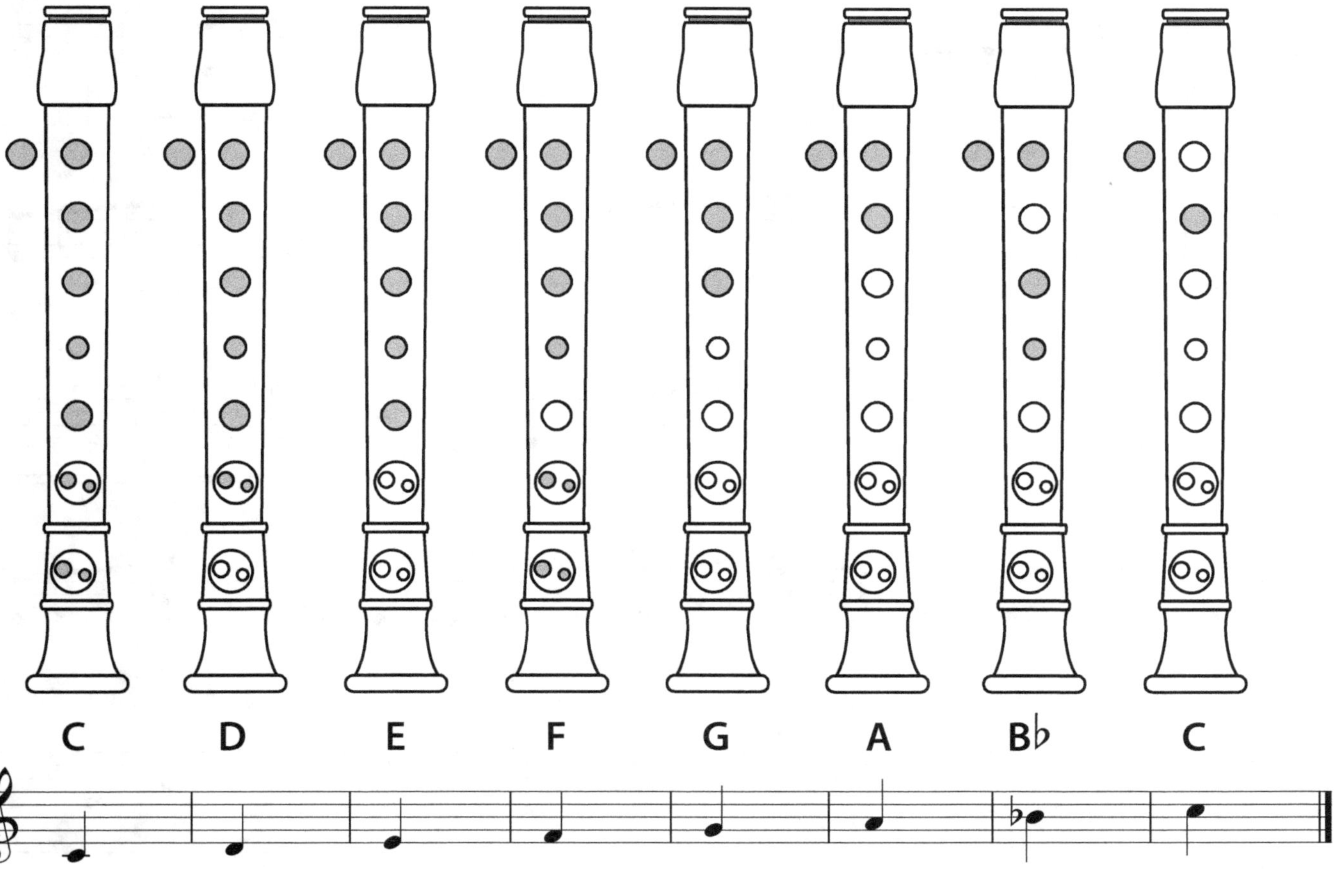

CARNIVAL OF THE ANIMALS FINALE

Camille Saint-Saëns (1835–1921)

Composed as a joke in 1894, *The Carnival of the Animals* is a suite of 14 short pieces with "Finale" as the last one. Each piece was composed for orchestra using a variety of instruments to mimic the sounds and movements of animals. Saint-Saëns couldn't have predicted the suite would still be popular 100 years after his death.

With Recorder, track 7
Recorder muted, track 8

Camille Saint-Saëns
Arranged by D. Carter

Medium Swing

$\quad$ = 90

Recorder

Image • Georgios Kollidas © 123RF.com

CARNIVAL OF THE ANIMALS FINALE

First play each note in the fingering diagram several times to become familiar. Set metronome to 4/4 time. Practice warm up and piece at 60 tempo. Slowly work your way to 90 tempo. "Finale" is in the key of D major. Every F and C are played as sharp. Follow the breath marks (') and blow even and relaxed air.

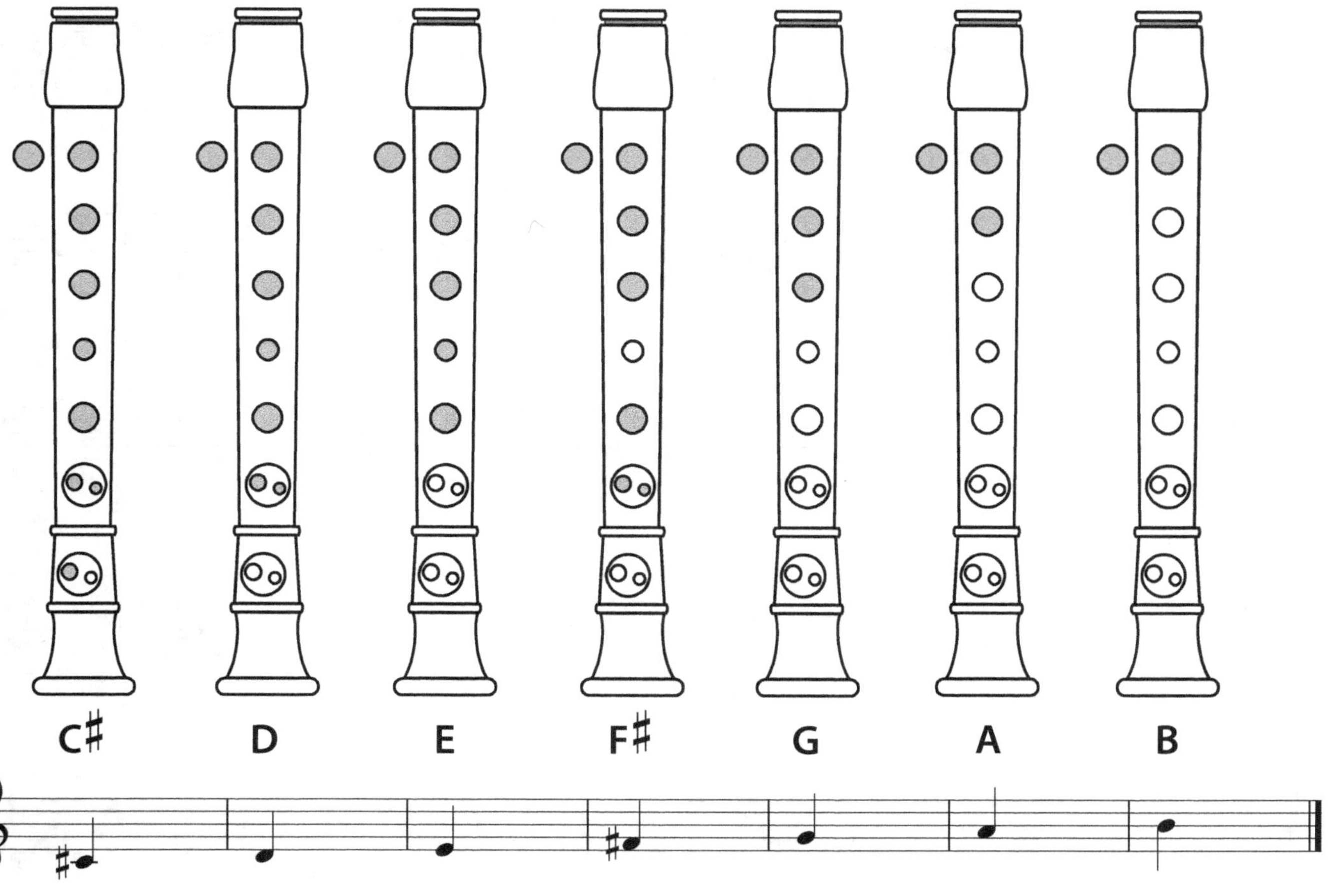

HUNGARIAN DANCE NO. 5

Johannes Brahms (1833–1897)

Though he was German, Brahms was influenced by Hungarian music at a young age. He worked as a piano accompanist performing Hungarian folk music. This inspired Brahms to compose 21 *Hungarian Dances*. "No. 5" is perhaps the most popular of the set.

With Recorder, track 9
Recorder muted, track 10

Johannes Brahms
Arranged by D. Carter

Image • Georgios Kollidas © 123RF.com

HUNGARIAN DANCE NO. 5

First play each note in the fingering diagram several times to become familiar. Do not cover both holes on RH 3rd finger E♭. Set metronome to 4/4 time. Practice warm up and piece at 55 tempo. Slowly work your way to 88 tempo. "Hungarian Dance No. 5" is in the key of G minor. Every B and E are played as flat. Follow the breath marks (') and blow even and relaxed air.

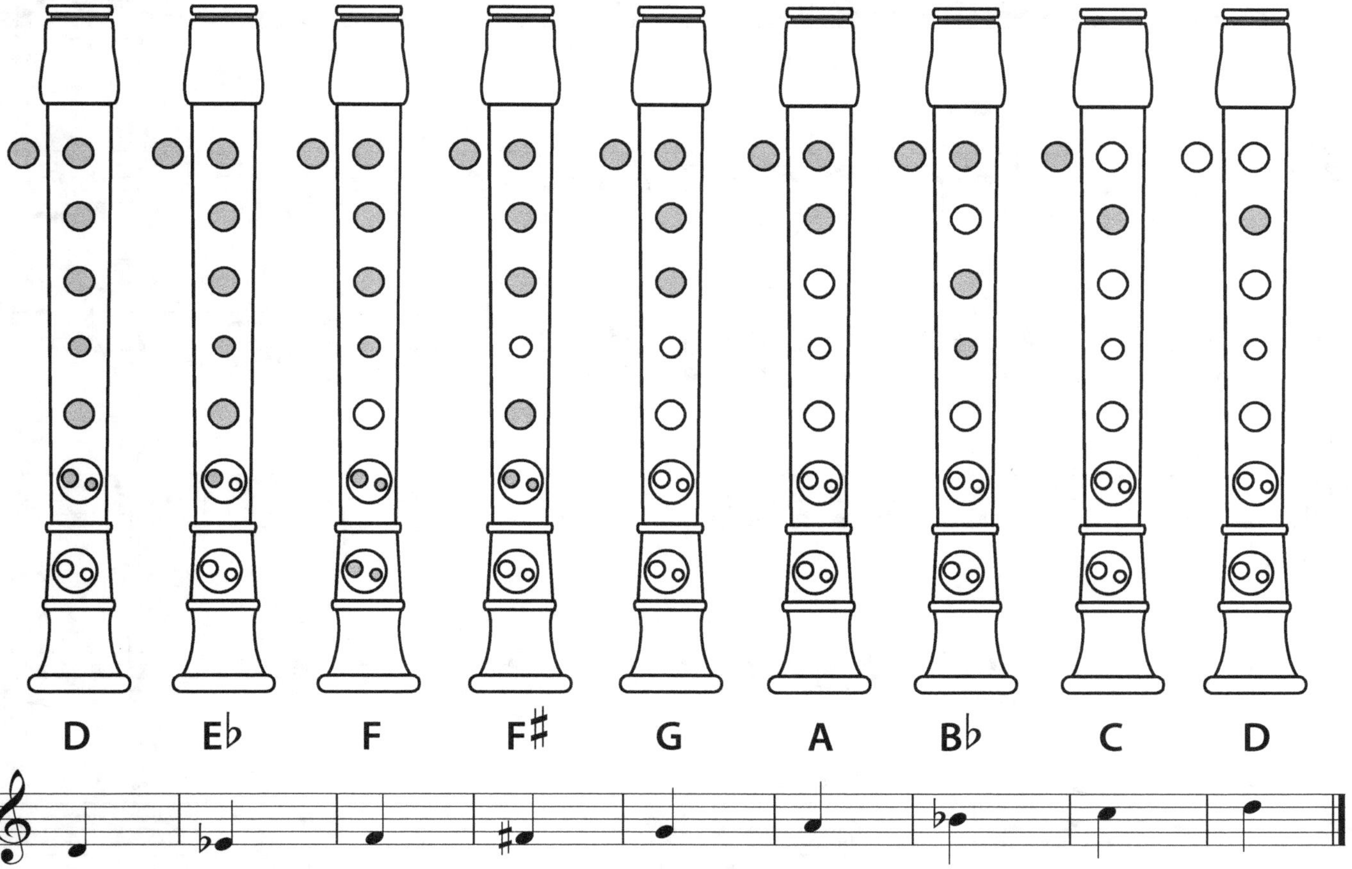

BARBER DE SEVILLE

Gioachino Rossini (1792–1868)

The Barber De Seville is Rossini's most famous opera. The first performance in 1816 was a failure. The audience booed, and a cat entered the stage during the show. The second performance was a success, and the opera became popular throughout Europe.

With Recorder, track 11
Recorder muted, track 12

Gioachino Rossini
Arranged by D. Carter

Image • Sergey Kohl © 123RF.com

Warm up

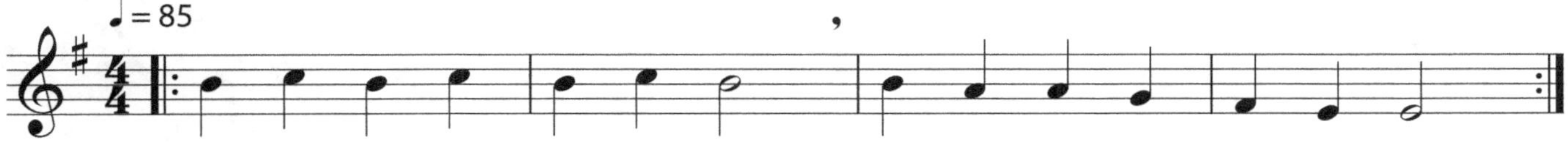

BARBER DE SEVILLE

First play each note in the fingering diagram several times to become familiar. Set metronome to 4/4 time. Practice warm up and piece at 85 tempo. Slowly work your way to 124 tempo. *Barber De Seville* is in the key of E minor. Every F is played as sharp. Follow the breath marks (') and blow even and relaxed air.

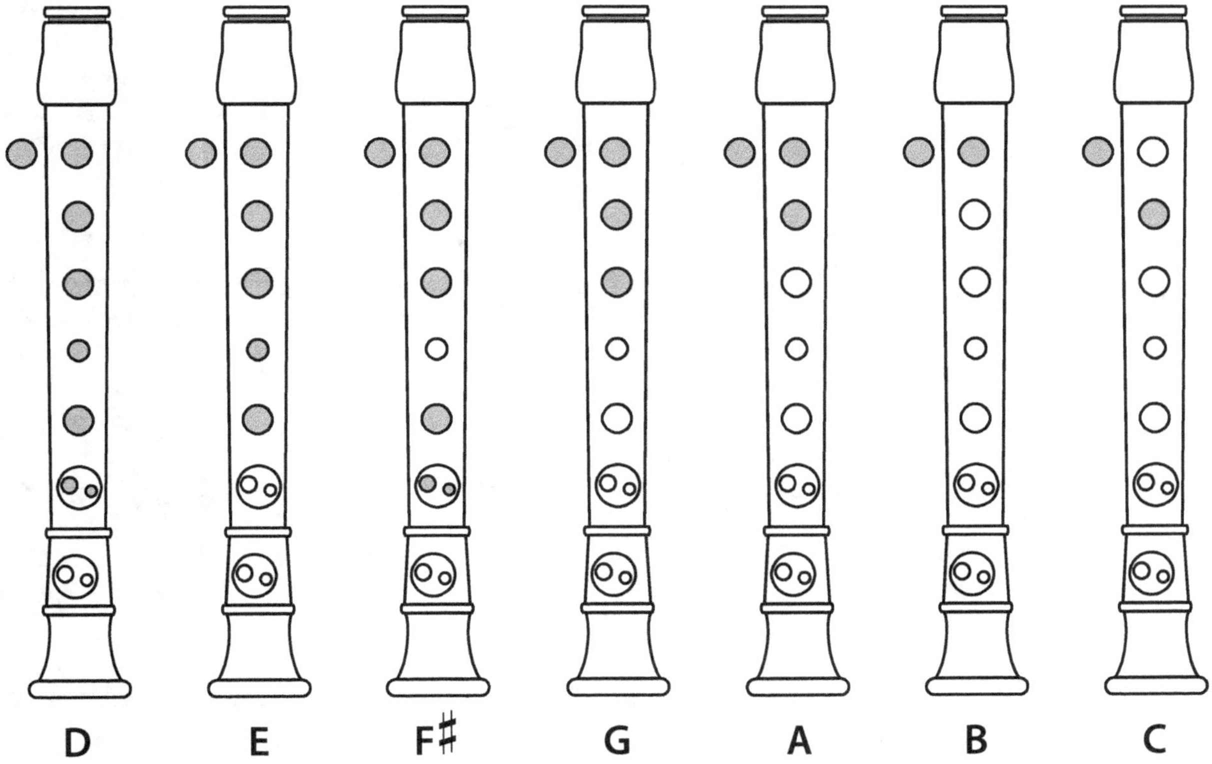

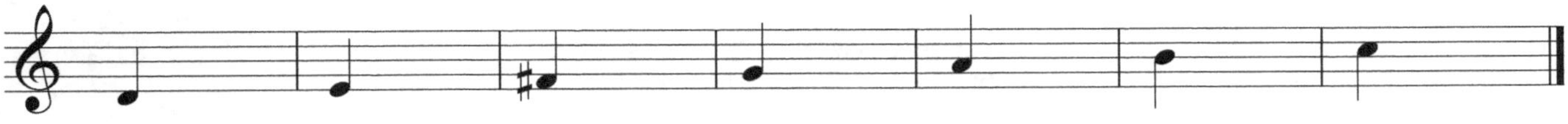

DANCE OF THE SUGARPLUM FAIRY

Pyotr Ilyich Tchaikovsky (1840–1893)

"Dance of the Sugar Plum Fairy" is the 3rd movement in *The Nutcracker* ballet composed by Tchaikovsky. The piece is very popular during the Christmas holidays. It premiered in 1892 and is danced by the principal female dancer.

With Recorder, track 13
Recorder muted, track 14

Pyotr Ilyich Tchaikovsky
Arranged by D. Carter

Image • Olga Popova © 123RF.com

Warm up

DANCE OF THE SUGAR PLUM FAIRY

First play each note in the fingering diagram several times to become familiar. Do not cover both holes on RH 3rd finger E♭. Set metronome to 4/4 time. Practice warm up and piece at 65 tempo. Slowly work your way to 85 tempo. "Dance of the Sugar Plum Fairy" is in the key of G minor. Every B and E are played as flat, however some of the Es are played natural. Follow the breath marks (') and blow even and relaxed air.

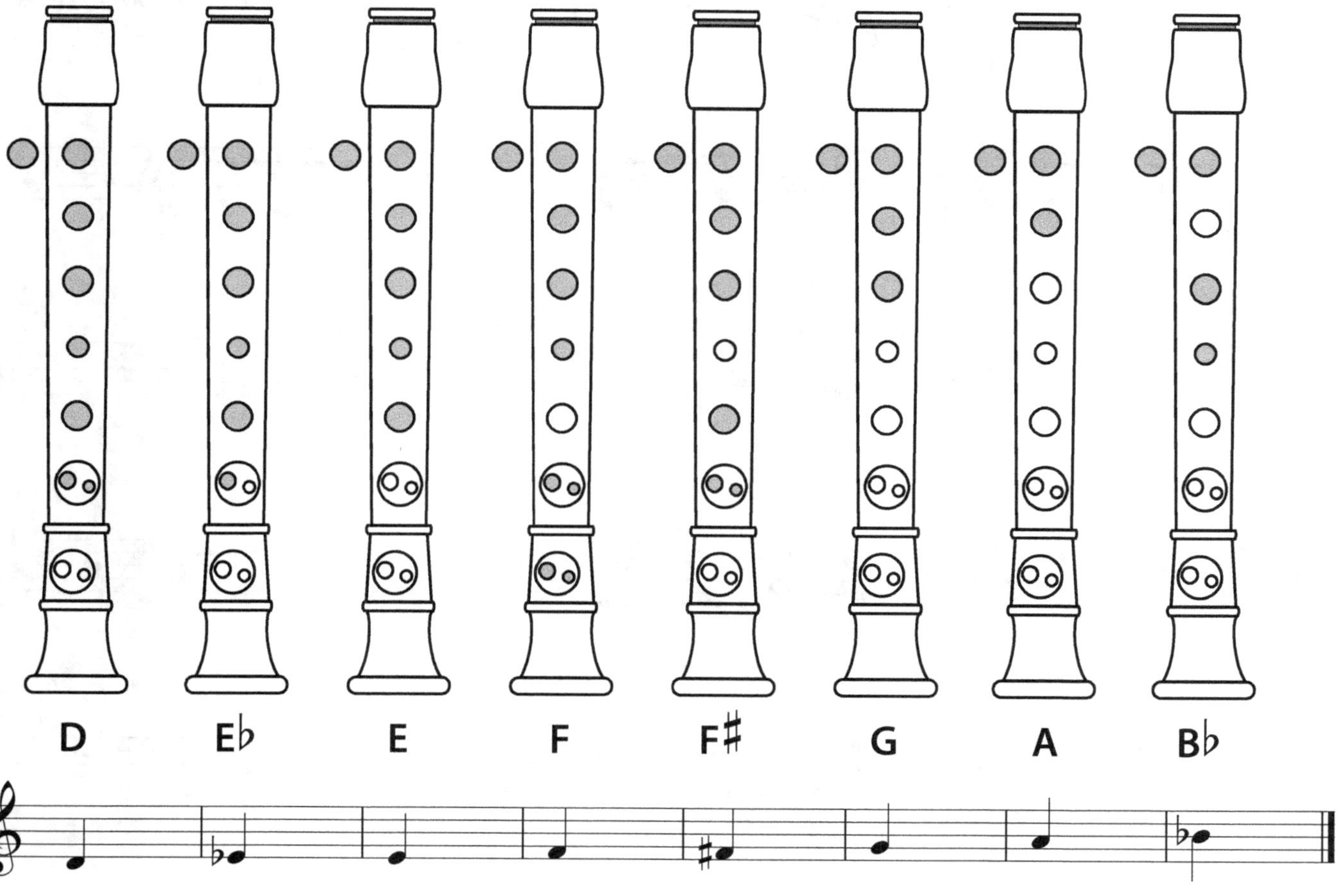

SYMPHONY NO. 40 IN G MINOR

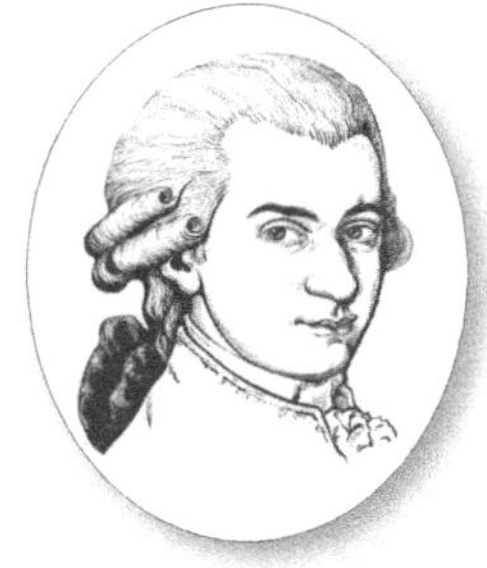

Wolfgang Amadeus Mozart (1756–1791)

Mozart composed *Symphony No. 40 In G Minor* in 1788. 1788 was a difficult year for Mozart. That may explain why this piece is one of only two of his symphonies written in minor keys.

With Recorder, track 15
Recorder muted, track 16

W. A. Mozart
Arranged by D. Carter

World Beat

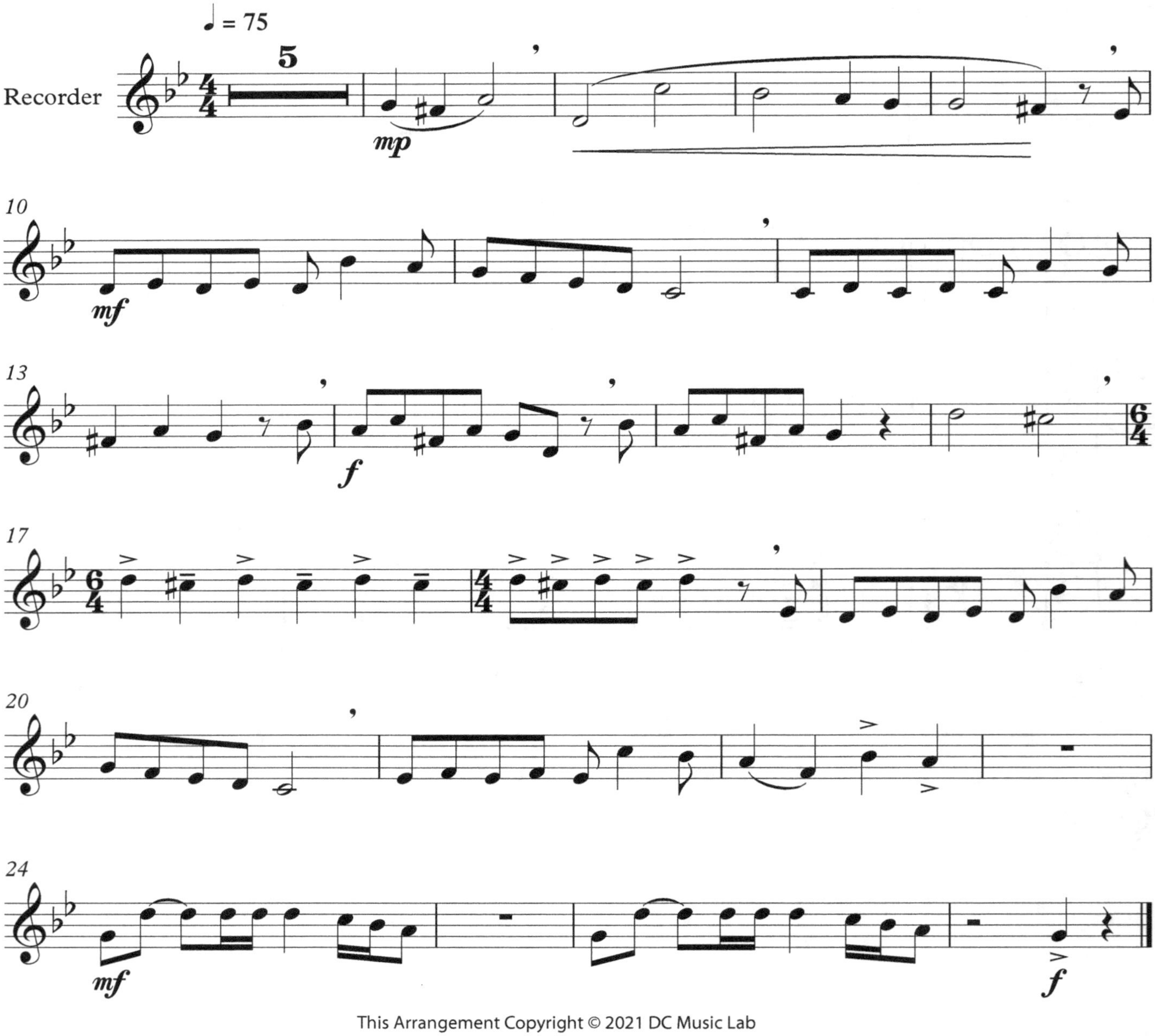

Image • Georgy Borozdkin © 123RF.com

SYMPHONY NO. 40 IN G MINOR

First play each note in the fingering diagram several times to become familiar. Practice sliding RH 3rd finger back and forth covering holes D and E♭. Set metronome to 4/4 time. Practice warm up and piece at 55 tempo. Slowly work your way to 75 tempo. *Symphony No. 40* is in the key of G minor. Every B and E are played as flat. Follow the breath marks (') and blow even and relaxed air.

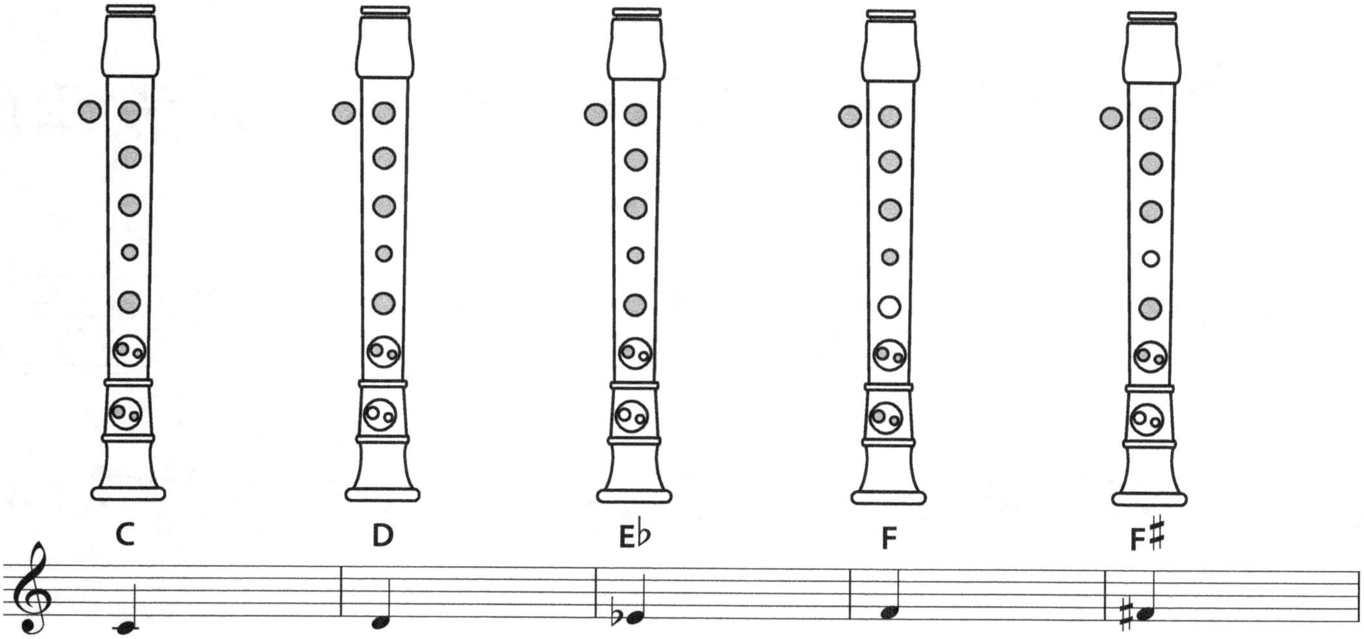

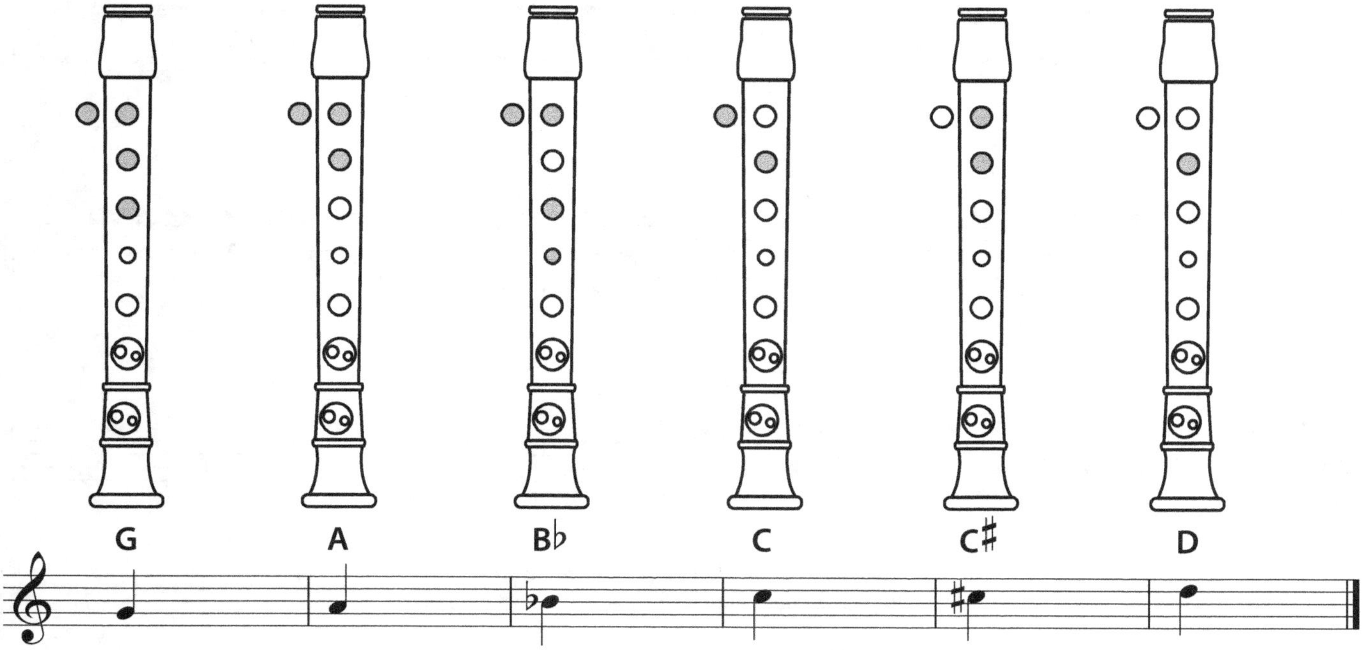

1812 OVERTURE

Pyotr Ilyich Tchaikovsky (1840–1893)

Tchaikovsky composed *1812 Overture* in 1880. It was to commemorate Russia's successful defense against Napoleon's army invasion in 1812. In 1974, The Boston Pops added real cannon blasts to the performance of this piece.

With Recorder, track 17
Recorder muted, track 18

Pyotr Ilyich Tchaikovsky
Arranged by D. Carter

Image • Olga Popova © 123RF.com

1812 OVERTURE

First play each note in the fingering diagram several times to become familiar. Practice high D and E back and forth with the thumb hole half open. Set metronome to 4/4 time. Practice warm up and piece at 50 tempo. *Isolate measures 16-19 to repeat practice.* Slowly work your way to 83 tempo. *1812 Overture* is in the key of G major. Every F is played as sharp. Follow the breath mark (') and blow even and relaxed air.

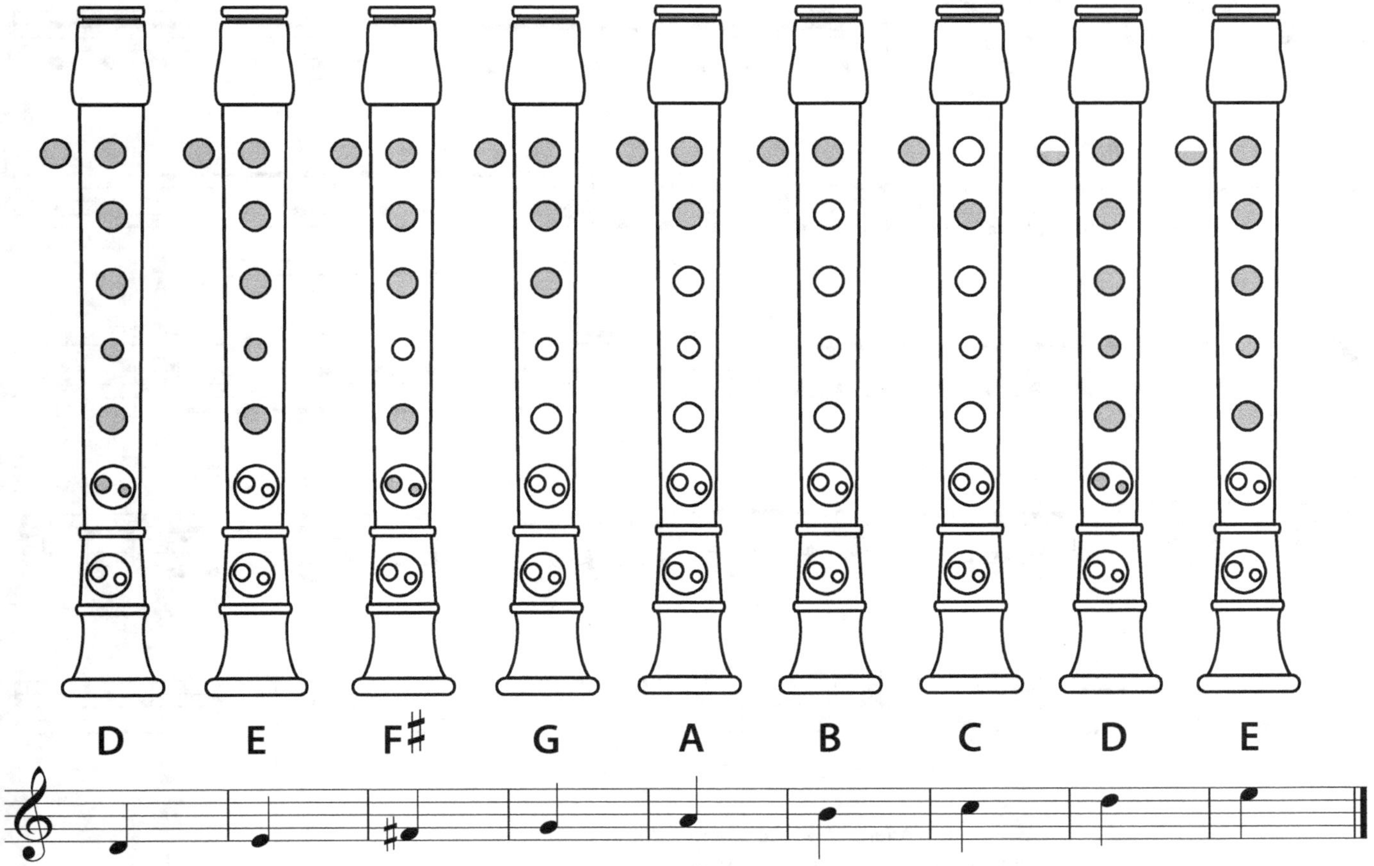

WINTER

Antonio Vivaldi (1678–1741)

Vivaldi was both a priest and a composer. "Winter" is one of four violin pieces he composed titled *The Four Seasons*, composed around 1723. Each piece is a musical expression of a season. Although *The Four Seasons* may be Vivaldi's most famous work, he composed an estimated 500 other pieces.

With Recorder, track 19
Recorder muted, track 20

Antonio Vivaldi
Arranged by D. Carter

Image • Georgy Borozdkin © 123RF.com

WINTER

First play each note in the fingering diagram several times to become familiar. Do not cover both holes on RH 3rd finger E♭. Do not cover both holes on RH 4th finger D♭. Do not cover both holes on RH 3rd finger A♭. Set metronome to 4/4 time. Practice warm up and piece at 50 tempo. Slowly work your way to 70 tempo. Follow the breath marks (') and blow even and relaxed air.

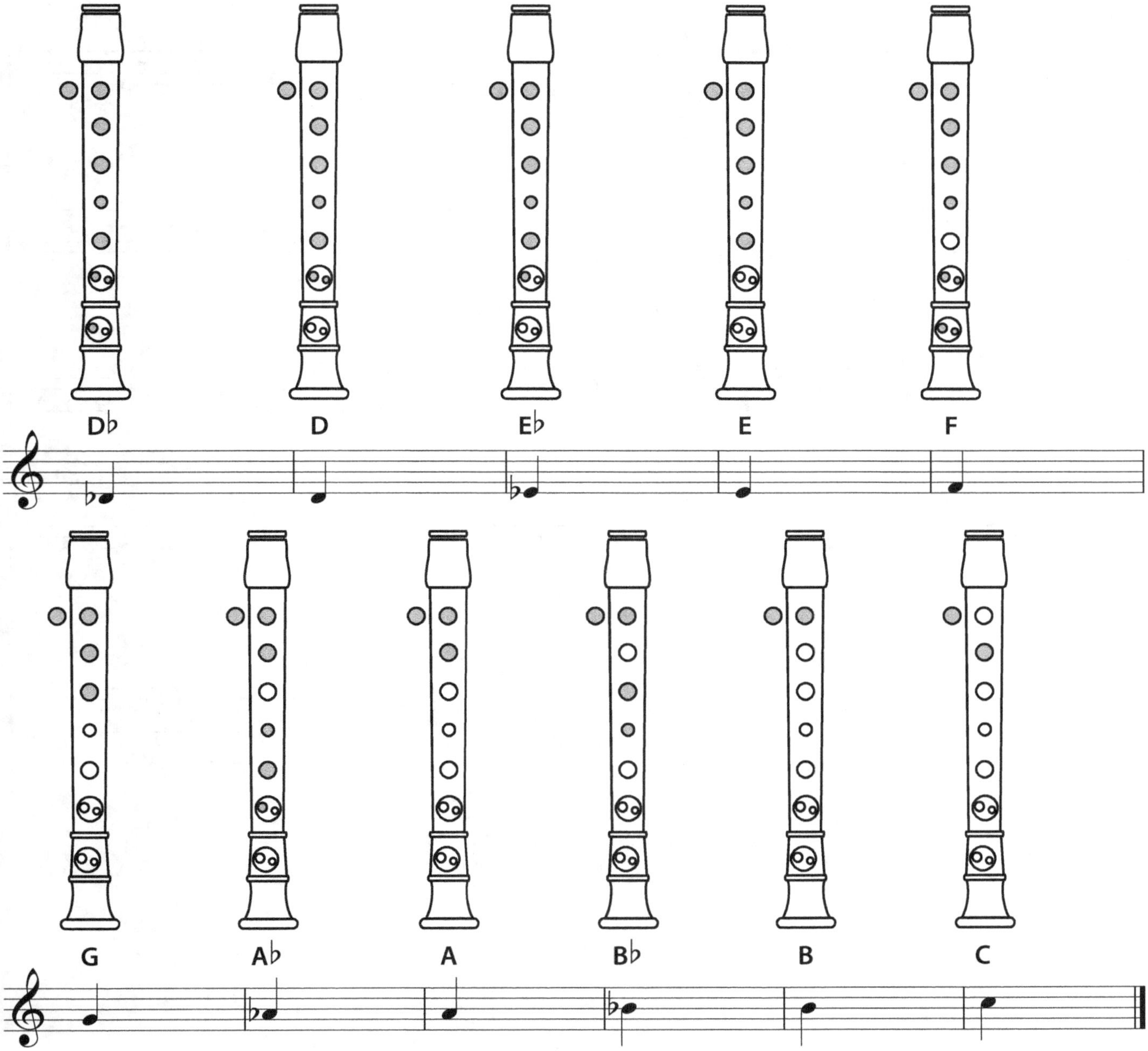

ROLLER SKATE ODYSSEY

Composed by Damon Carter, "Roller Skate, Odyssey" revisits the combining of Disco music with roller skating from the 1970s and 1980s. The popularity of roller skating is on the rise again.

With Recorder, track 21
Recorder muted, track 22

D. Carter

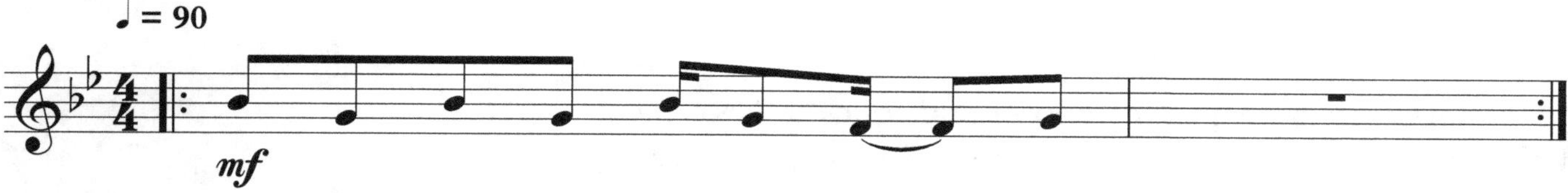

ROLLER SKATE ODYSSEY

First play each note in the fingering diagram several times to become familiar. Set metronome to 4/4 time. Practice warm up and piece at 90 tempo. "Roller Skate Odyssey" is in the key of G minor. Every B and E are played as flat. However, there are no Es in this song. Slowly work your way to 120 tempo. Follow the breath marks (') and blow even and relaxed air.

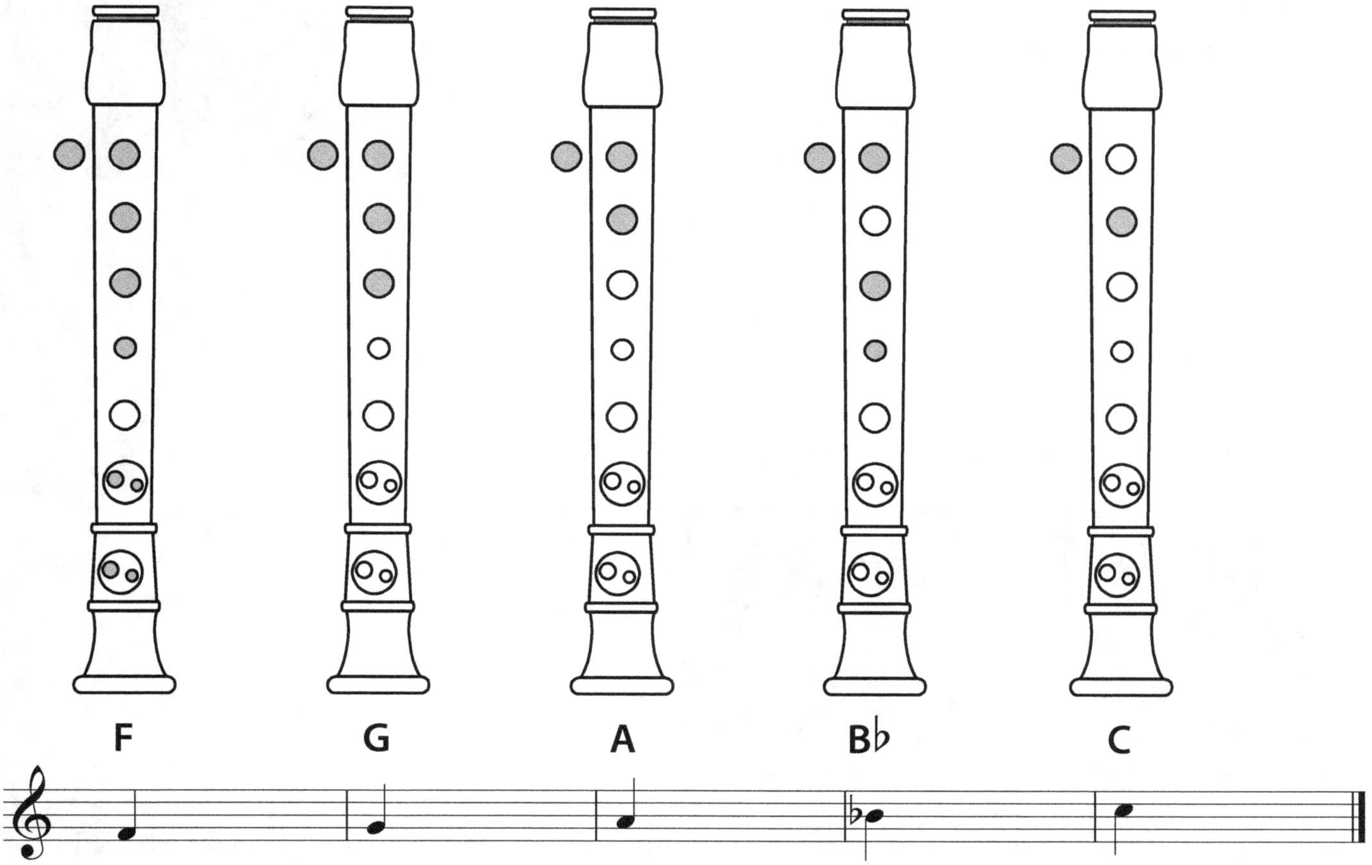

About the Author

Damon Carter is a pianist, composer, and educator. His career spans over 20 years as a private piano instructor, and K-12 music teacher in public schools. Damon earned his Bachelor of Music Degree in Performance from Berklee College of Music in Boston, MA. He then went on to earn a Master of Education Degree from Cambridge College in Cambridge, MA.

In addition to music education, Damon's career as a professional pianist has also thrived for many years. He has performed at hundreds of weddings, corporate events, recordings, restaurant venues, and concerts. Most recently, Damon has added author to his resume with the launch of DC Music Lab's premier release *Classical Remix For The Recorder*.

To learn more:

- Visit
  www.dcmusiclab.com and *www.cal-premier.com*

- To listen to the selections in this book in their original form, type the titles into the search field on *www.youtube.com*.